FLEX-ABILITY
HOLIDAY

Solo-Duet-Trio-Quartet With Optional Accompaniment

NEW YEAR'S EVE

Arranged by VICTOR LÓPEZ

CONTENTS

(0690B) OBOE/GUITAR (MELODY)/PIANO/
  GUITAR CHORDS/ELECTRIC BASS
(0691B) FLUTE
(0692B) CLARINET/BASS CLARINET
(0693B) ALTO SAX/BARITONE SAX
(0694B) TENOR SAX
(0695B) TRUMPET/BARITONE T.C.
(0696B) HORN IN F
(0697B) TROMBONE/BARITONE/BASSOON/TUBA
(0698B) VIOLIN
(0699B) VIOLA
(0700B) CELLO/BASS
(0701B) PERCUSSION (MALLET SOLO, MALLET HARMONY,
  AUXILIARY PERCUSSION, DRUM SET (SNARE, BASS, CYMBALS))
(0702B) CD ACCOMPANIMENT

Project Manager/Editor: Thom Proctor
Cover Design: Ernesto Ebanks and Candy Woolley
CD MIDI Sequencing: Mike Lewis

JINGLE BELLS

TRADITIONAL
Arranged by VICTOR LÓPEZ

PERCUSSION

SANTA CLAUS IS COMIN' TO TOWN

Words by HAVEN GILLESPIE
Music by J. FRED COOTS
Arranged by VICTOR LÓPEZ

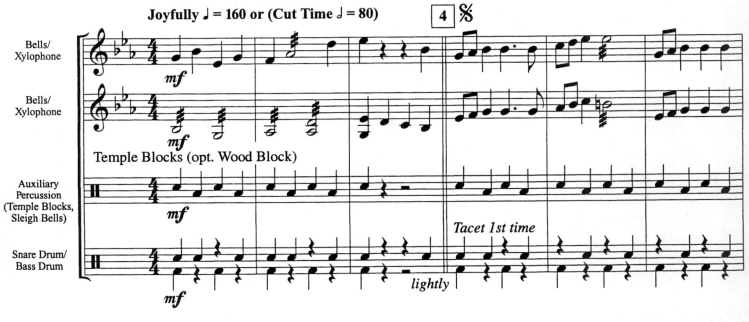

HAVE YOURSELF A MERRY LITTLE CHRISTMAS

Words and Music by
HUGH MARTIN and RALPH BLANE
Arranged by VICTOR LÓPEZ

(I'm Gettin') NUTTIN' FOR CHRISTMAS

Words and Music by
SID TEPPER and ROY C. BENNETT
Arranged by VICTOR LÓPEZ

FROSTY THE SNOWMAN

Words and Music by
STEVE NELSON and
JACK ROLLINS
Arranged by VICTOR LÓPEZ

I'LL BE HOME FOR CHRISTMAS

Words by KIM GANNON
Music by WALTER KENT
Arranged by VICTOR LÓPEZ

D.S. %̸ al Coda   ⊕ *Coda*

Susp. Cym.

Cr. Cyms.

0701B

ANGELS WE HAVE HEARD ON HIGH

TRADITIONAL
Arranged by VICTOR LÓPEZ

JOY TO THE WORLD

TRADITIONAL
Arranged by VICTOR LÓPEZ

WE WISH YOU A MERRY CHRISTMAS

TRADITIONAL
Arranged by VICTOR LÓPEZ

AULD LANG SYNE

TRADITIONAL
Arranged by VICTOR LÓPEZ

CHANUKAH /I HAVE A LITTLE DREYDL

TRADITIONAL
Arranged by VICTOR LÓPEZ

FLEX-ABILITY SERIES

Solo-duet-trio-quartet or any small or large ensemble
Woodwinds, brass, strings, percussion

You can play together in harmony with classmates, family, and friends, with any combination of instruments, from less than one year of lessons to two, three, or more years of playing ability. Everybody can play!

Top line	Melody	Level 2½ to 3	Intermediate-level range; sixteenth-note combinations; rock/jazz syncopations
Second line	Harmony	Level 2 to 2½	Wider range; up to sixteenth notes; easy syncopations
Third line	Harmony	Level 1½	Limited range; up to eighth notes
Bottom line	Harmony or bass line	Level 1	Narrow range; whole, half, and quarter notes; easy key and time signatures

The CD accompaniment is available separately. Each song has two tracks: one with a full demonstration performance and one with just the rhythm section for you to play along as a solo, duet, trio, quartet, or larger ensemble.

FLEX-ABILITY
HOLIDAY   Arranged by VICTOR LÓPEZ

TITLES:
Jingle Bells
Santa Claus Is Comin' to Town
Have Yourself a Merry Little Christmas
(I'm Gettin') Nuttin' for Christmas
Frosty the Snowman
I'll Be Home for Christmas
Angels We Have Heard on High
Joy to the World
We Wish You a Merry Christmas
Auld Lang Syne
Chanukah Medley:
  Chanukah/I Have a Little Dreydl

INSTRUMENTATION:
(0690B) OBOE/GUITAR (MELODY)/PIANO/
  GUITAR CHORDS/ELECTRIC BASS
(0691B) FLUTE
(0692B) CLARINET/BASS CLARINET
(0693B) ALTO SAX/BARITONE SAX
(0694B) TENOR SAX
(0695B) TRUMPET/BARITONE T.C.
(0696B) HORN IN F
(0697B) TROMBONE/BARITONE/BASSOON/TUBA
(0698B) VIOLIN
(0699B) VIOLA
(0700B) CELLO/BASS
(0701B) PERCUSSION (MALLET SOLO,
  MALLET HARMONY, AUXILIARY PERCUSSION,
  DRUM SET [SNARE, BASS, CYMBALS])
(0702B) CD ACCOMPANIMENT

alfred.com

ISBN-10: 0-7579-0850-0
ISBN-13: 978-0-7579-0850-7

0701B $7.99

ISBN 0-7579-0850-0

T4-AXP-490

STORYTELLER: They gazed into the sky and noticed that one star shone more brightly than all the others. *(Starholder enters and carries the star toward the stage.)* One extraordinary star.

8. BEAUTIFUL STAR OF BETHLEHEM

(from "A Simple Christmas Pageant")

Arranged by SHELDON CURRY

Words and Music by
ADGER M. PACE *and* R. FISHER BOYCE

STORYTELLER: They gently gathered to get a closer look at Jesus.

9. AWAY IN A MANGER
(from "A Simple Christmas Pageant")

Words: Anon. (Luke 2:7)

Music by **JAMES R. MURRAY**
Arranged by **SHELDON CURRY**

A - way in a man-ger no crib for a bed, the
lit - tle Lord Je - sus laid down his sweet head. The stars in the sky___ looked
down where he lay, the lit - tle Lord Je - sus a - sleep on the hay.___

STORYTELLER: They were drawn by the great light too, and set out to discover more about it.

10. WE THREE KINGS
(from "A Simple Christmas Pageant")

Arranged by **SHELDON CURRY**

Words and Music by
John Henry Hopkins, Jr.

1. We three kings of O - ri - ent
2. Born a king on Beth - le - hem's
3. Frank - in - cense to of - fer have
4. Myrrh is mine; its bit - ter per -
5. Glo - rious now be - hold he is

are bear - ing gifts we tra - verse a - far; field and
plain, gold I bring to crown him a - gain, King for
I: in - cense owns a De - i - ty nigh; prayer and
fume breathes a life of gath - er - ing gloom; sor - rowing,
born, King, Re - deem - er, God's gra - cious Son; heav'n sings

foun - tain moor and moun - tain fol - low - ing yon - der star.
ev - er ceas - ing nev - er o - ver us all to reign.
prais - ing, glad - ly rais - ing, wor - ship him, God Most High.
sigh - ing, bleed - ing, dy - ing, sealed in the stone - cold tomb.
al - le - lu - ia, al - le - lu - ia we join as one.

O___ star of won - der, star of night, star with ro - yal beau - ty

bright; west - ward lead - ing still pro - ceed - ing guide us to thy per - fect light!

STORYTELLER: And now, ladies and gentlemen, let's all stand and give greetings to one another. "The Peace of the Lord be with you." *(general commotion as people stand, mingle and greet each other. After an appropriate amount of time, the Storyteller brings order and continues.)* May God richly bless you and Merry, Merry Christmas everyone! Thank you children, thank you grown-ups, thank you St. Nicholas, and thanks to everyone for being a part of "A Simple Christmas Pageant". How about singing one last carol together, shall we?

11. GO TELL IT ON THE MOUNTAIN

(from "A Simple Christmas Pageant")

Arranged by **SHELDON CURRY**

19th c. African American Spiritual
(Words: alt. SC)

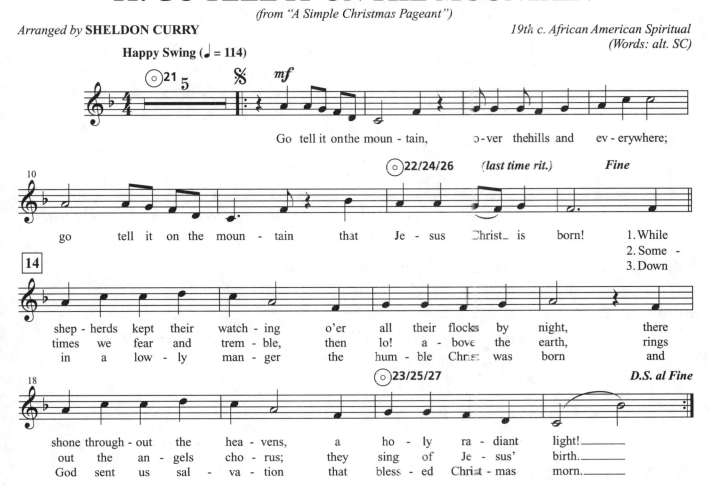

SCENE ONE: THE VISITOR

[The Storyteller moves to the appointed mark and begins …]

STORYTELLER: An amazing night. A simple Nativity play to remember the story. Our church family gathered to sing carols and light candles and bathe in the warmth of Christmas. Can something so plain pay homage to an event so spectacular? Yes, it can. This year, maybe more than ever, we need a simple Christmas pageant. So, welcome! Welcome, friends and family and special guests...welcome and Merry Christmas!

CONGREGATION: Merry Christmas!

STORYTELLER: I'm delighted you're here. We have worked hard to prepare "A Simple Christmas Pageant". I'll tell the story adapted from the Gospel of Luke while actors play out the events that lead to the manger...but first, a question? Who comes to visit us at Christmas? Anyone?

CONGREGATION: *(any answers work, but these answers are heard from some in the audience)* Jesus! Santa Claus! Nanna and Peepaw!

STORYTELLER: Well, yes and yes and yes again! The story of Christmas is full of surprises and unexpected visitors, and when we stop to *(interrupted by the sound of sleigh bells from offstage)* Wait … did you hear something … or someone? Who could it be?

CONGREGATION: *(any answers work, but these answers are heard from some in the audience)* Jesus! Santa Claus! Rudolph! Nanna and Peepaw!

STORYTELLER: Only one way to find out. All right boys and girls and grownups, can you be as quiet as a snowflake falling to the ground? Let's try...shhh – shhh...good, good...shhh – shhh *(stage whisper)*...now listen, listen *(sleigh bells louder, still offstage – St. Nicholas enters)*

Oh my goodness! *(to St. Nicholas)* Greetings, sir. And what is your name?

ST. NICHOLAS: I am Nicholas, Bishop of Myra *(bowing to the Storyteller and the audience)*.

STORYTELLER: Oh, I thought maybe you were Santa Claus.

ST. NICHOLAS: Some people call me that.

STORYTELLER: I'm confused. Saint Nicholas? Santa Claus? Which is it?

ST. NICHOLAS: Not to worry, my friend. I'm happy to explain, but *(fully noticing the audience)* you seem to be in the middle of some special event. I don't want to intrude.

STORYTELLER: Oh no, you're not intruding! Everyone is welcome here. You're right, though, this a special event. It's "A Simple Christmas Pageant". But come. Tell us *your* story, then we'll tell you ours.

ST. NICHOLAS: Thank you for your kindness. *(taking in the scene)* I'm always happy to share my story. *(pause)* I was born in the Middle East, ages ago in the ancient city of Myra. The spirit of Christmas was real in those days, too. You see, back then, the story was only a few hundred years old. Not thousands like it is for you!

STORYTELLER: Who first told you of Jesus' birth?

ST. NICHOLAS: Like many of you, my parents told me. I loved to hear about the incredible birth and about Jesus' childhood and ministry. The faith of my mother and father led me to become a priest. But sadly, both my parents died when I was young. I felt empty inside. As an inheritance, they left me lots of silver and gold, but none of it brought me joy.

STORYTELLER: What did you do?

ST. NICHOLAS: I did what Christ had done. I gave my belongings to the poor. I comforted the sick and lonely. I loved children with all my heart. It was my joy and privilege to serve as the Bishop of Myra until one day... *(sighing)* one day, an evil ruler came to power. I was thrown into prison because I refused to deny Jesus.

STORYTELLER: You went to jail because you were Christian?

ST. NICHOLAS: Yes, but not just me. Many others, too. My faith helped me survive years of hard, sad times. When at last I was freed, I looked like the old man I was – with this long beard to show for it! *(stroking his beard)*

STORYTELLER: So you *ARE* Saint Nicholas?

ST. NICHOLAS: Indeed, I am.

STORYTELLER: And all your life you gave gifts as a way to mirror the love of Christ?

ST. NICHOLAS: *(gathering strength)* Yes, I did. Jesus the Christ, the Prince of peace, the King of kings, the Baby in the manger became for me – the Gift of all gifts. His life should be the reason we celebrate Christmas; we must never forget that. But please, your event is not about me – what did you call it? A Simple Christmas Pageant? I'd love to see it.

STORYTELLER: Oh, my – with Saint Nicholas as our special guest? The pleasure is all ours, I promise. *(turning to face the audience)* Children, family, friends, and Unexpected Guests, *(smiling to St. Nicholas)* we now present "A Simple Christmas Pageant"! Please join us singing carols and watch as the journey to Bethlehem unfolds.

SCENE TWO: THE ANGEL

[The Storyteller lifts the "Christmas Story" book in a manner so that all can see what it is and places it on a stand. He slowly opens the book and begins to read.]

STORYTELLER: Once upon a time, more long ago than you can imagine, the world seemed dark and hopeless. Romans had conquered and ruled Israel. Ancient prophets promised a Savior – a Messiah. The Jewish people prayed that God would send their beloved king soon. Their lives were filled with misery.

HYMN: *(All singing)* **"O Come, O Come Emmanuel"**

STORYTELLER: One day, a devout young girl named Mary was walking, saying her prayers in her garden in Nazareth. All of a sudden, she saw a bright light! *(Mary reacts to light)* What could it be? She had no idea. An angel appeared to Mary! *(Mary reacts to Gabriel's gestures and mimed speech)* The Angel told Mary that God had chosen her to be the mother of the long-awaited Messiah.

HYMN: *(All singing)* **"The Angel Gabriel From Heaven Came"**

STORYTELLER: Nearby lived a carpenter named Joseph. He was a man of great faith and loved Mary with all his heart. They planned to be married. One night, the same Angel that Mary

A Simple Christmas Pageant

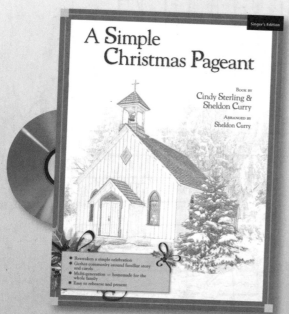

A Simple Christmas Pageant is a multi-generational Christmas program. It is brief (35 minutes), intentionally simple and reminiscent of a slower gentler time (think "A Prairie Home Companion" meets "A Charlie Brown Christmas"). There are only two speaking parts; A **Storyteller and Saint Nicholas**. Cindy Sterling and Sheldon Curry have created a hassle-free, inexpensive alternative to big Christmas musicals. It requires little rehearsal time, few financial resources and is family friendly. The music and carols are familiar, and the congregation sings along with every piece. It is intended for folks who want to provide a relaxed Christmas program the whole neighborhood will attend and enjoy. *A Simple Christmas Pageant* is sure to become a warm, community-building Christmas worship tradition.

Director's Score	00-32332
Preview Pack	00-32337
Singer's Edition	00-32338
Listening CD	00-32335
Bulk CD Set	00-32336
InstruTrax CD	00-32334
InstruPax	00-32333
Bulletin Insert	00-32339

- Offers a simplified approach to a Christmas program
- Includes traditional carols and familiar stories
- Easy to practice and present
- Appropriate for all ages

ALSO AVAILABLE:

Evening in December

A Carol Fantasia

O Come, Emmanuel

32338 Singer's Edition   US $3.95

0 38081 34742 4

alfred.com

ISBN-10: 0-7390-6299-9
ISBN-13: 978-0-7390-6299-9

9 780739 062999

503

To my friend Brett, who brought the journey home

Tango salvaje de Mendoza

"Wild Tango from Mendoza"

In Mendoza, Argentina, locals gather late in the evening and into the early hours of the morning to celebrate the tango. This traditional form of music and dance is known for its passionate execution.

Rhythm Workshop

Tap rhythm 3x daily.

mm. 15–16

Primo

Wynn-Anne Rossi

Passionately! ($\quad$ = 112)

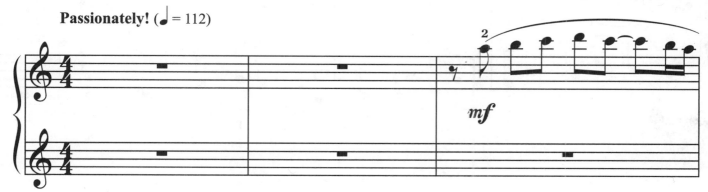

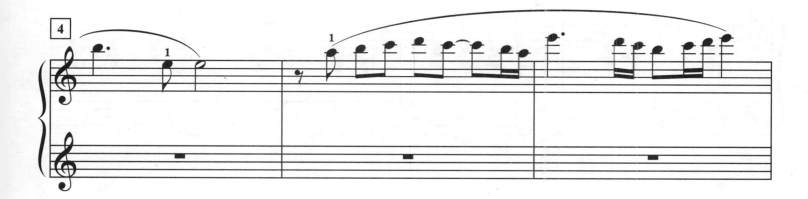

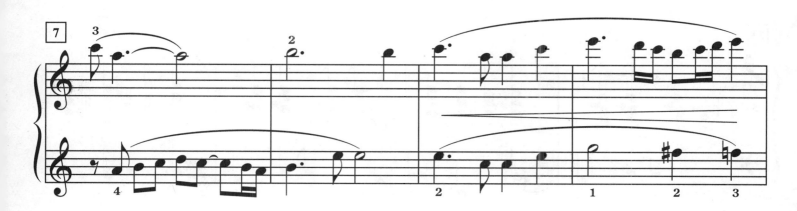

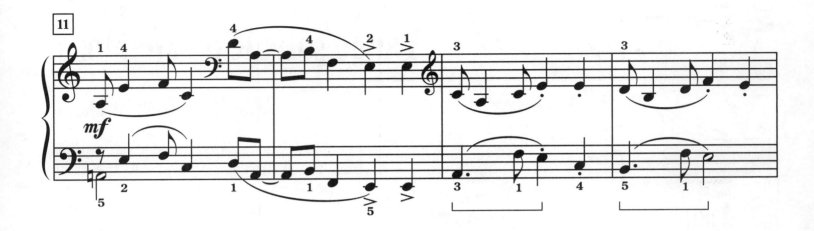

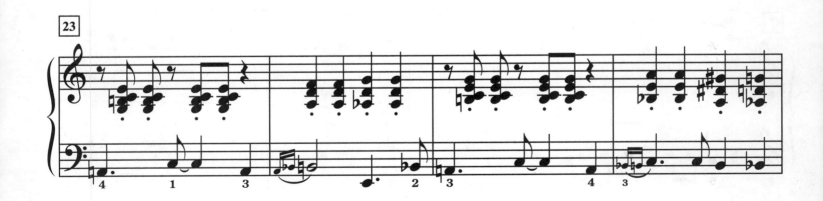

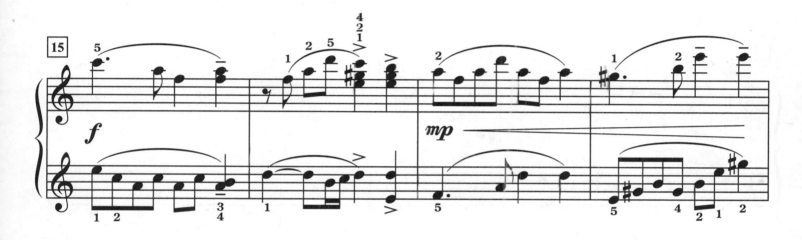

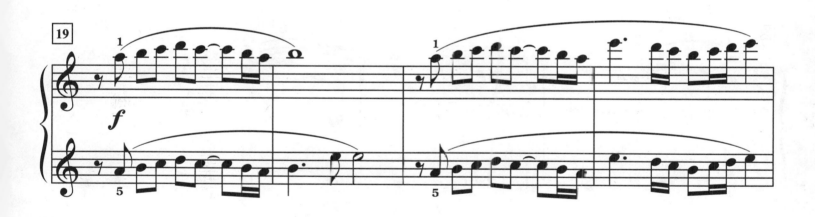

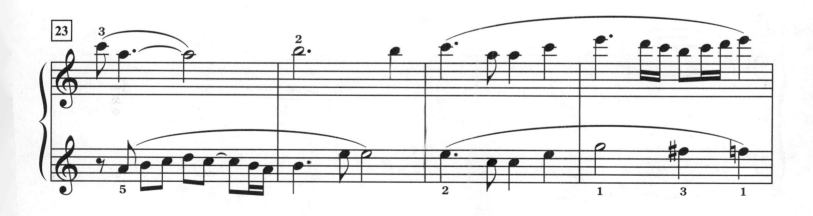

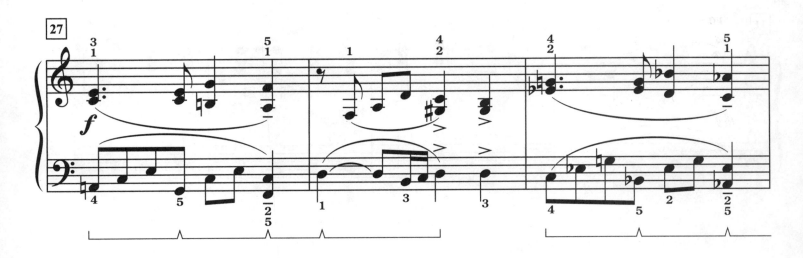

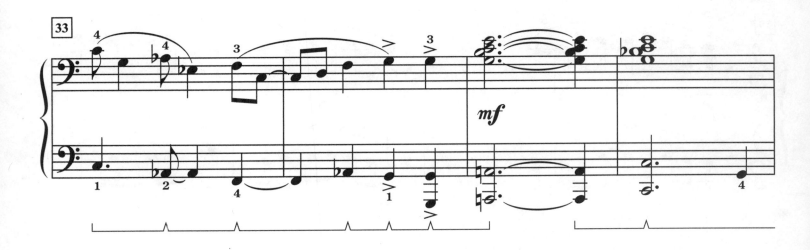

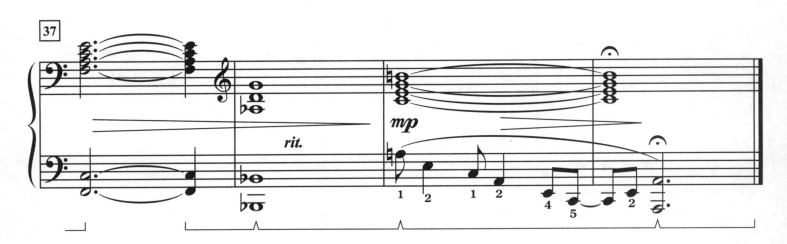

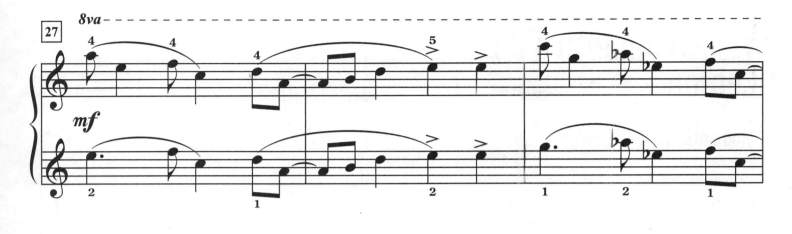

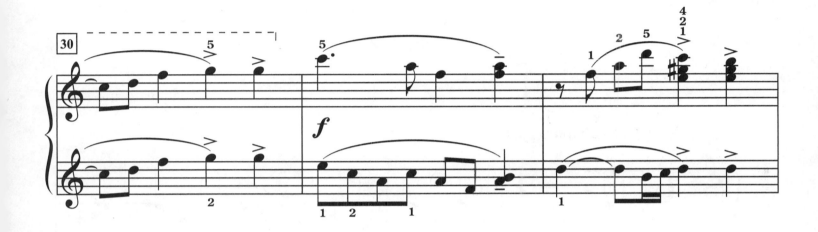

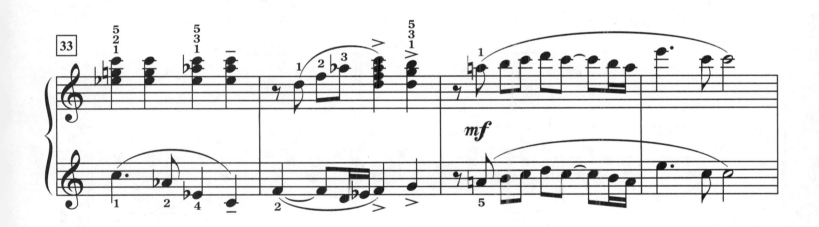

Visão romântica do Leblon

"Romantic View of Leblon"

A hike up one of the twin peaks of Dois Irmãos (Twin Brothers) in Rio de Janeiro, Brazil, offers a beautiful bird's-eye view of Leblon Beach. It is a romantic spot to share a sunrise.

Rhythm Workshop

Tap rhythm 3x daily.

mm. 1–2

Secondo

Wynn-Anne Rossi

Relaxed and happy (♩ = 120)

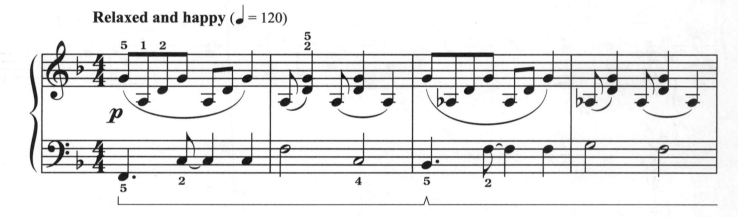

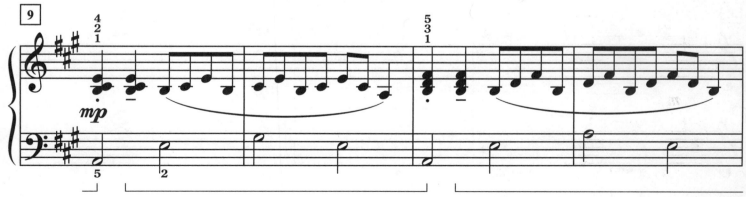

Visão romântica do Leblon

"Romantic View of Leblon"

A hike up one of the twin peaks of Dois Irmãos (Twin Brothers) in Rio de Janeiro, Brazil, offers a beautiful bird's-eye view of Leblon Beach. It is a romantic spot to share a sunrise.

Rhythm Workshop

Tap rhythm 3x daily.

mm. 17–18

Primo

Wynn-Anne Rossi

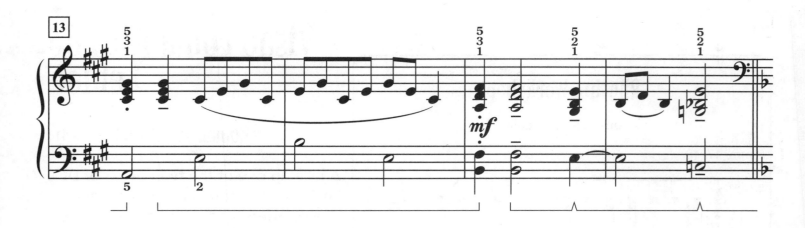

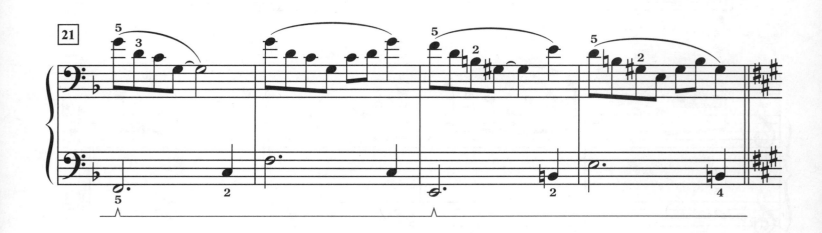

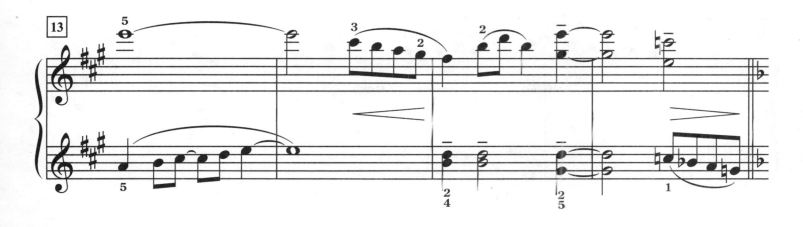

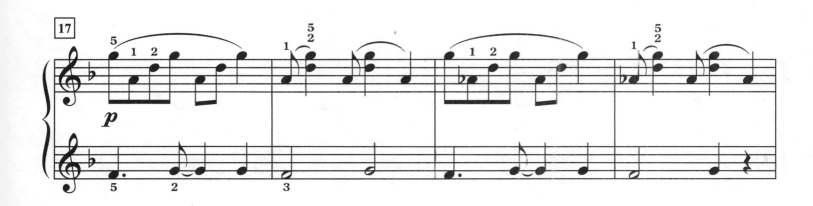

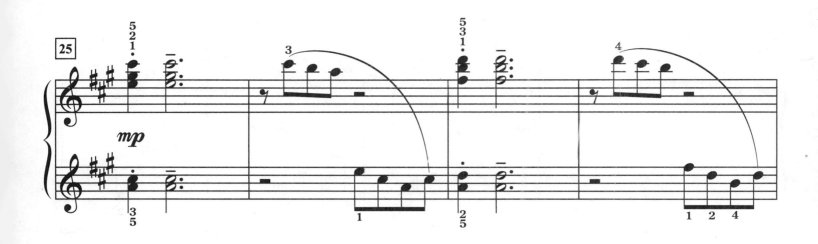

Secondo

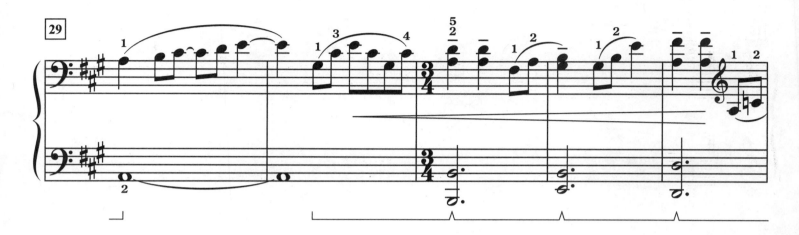

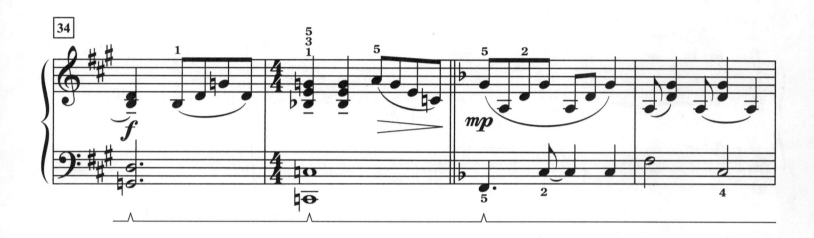

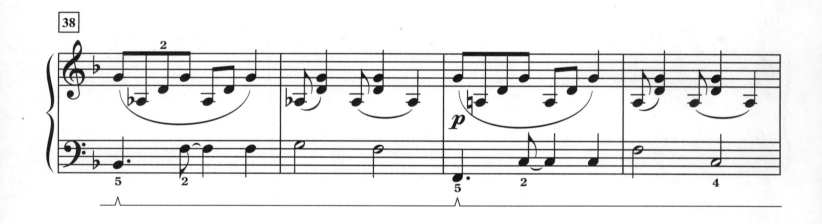

Cha-cha auténtica

"Authentic Cha-cha"

Authentic Cuban Cha-cha does not start on beat one! Dancers are challenged to skip the downbeat and begin the step pattern on beat two. Cha-cha is counted as "2–3–4–and–1" or "2–3–cha-cha-cha."

Rhythm Workshop

Tap rhythm 3x daily.

mm. 9–10

Secondo

Wynn-Anne Rossi

Emphasizing beat 2 (♩ = 120)

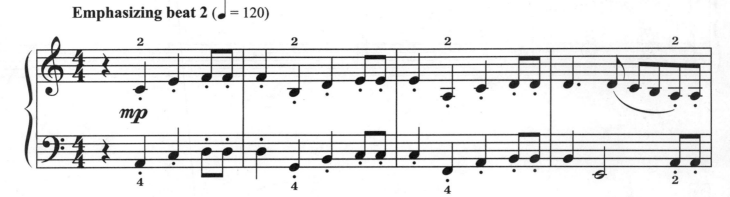

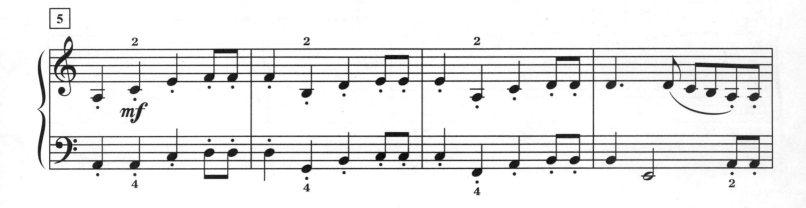

Cha-cha auténtica

"Authentic Cha-cha"

Authentic Cuban Cha-cha does not start on beat one! Dancers are challenged to skip the downbeat and begin the step pattern on beat two. Cha-cha is counted as "2–3–4–and–1" or "2–3–cha-cha-cha."

Rhythm Workshop

Tap rhythm 3x daily.

mm. 13–14

Primo

Wynn-Anne Rossi

Emphasizing beat 2 ($\quad$ = 120)

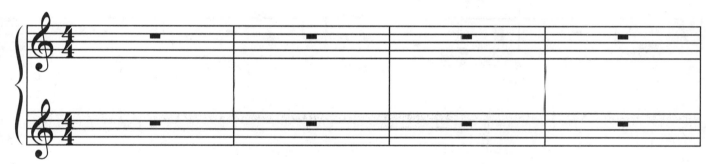

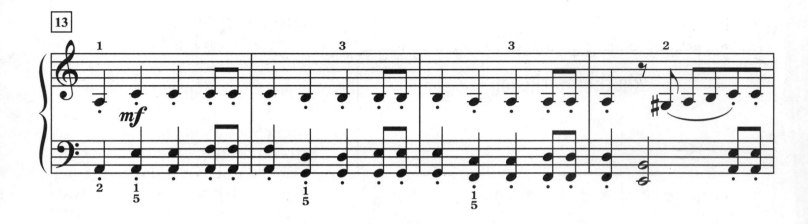

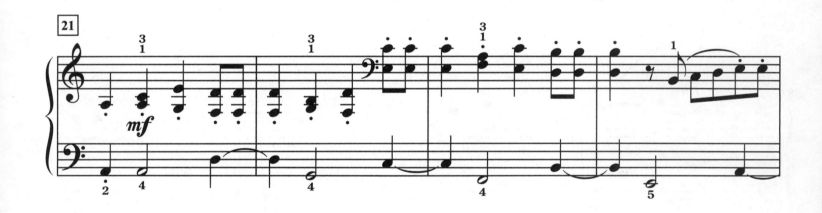

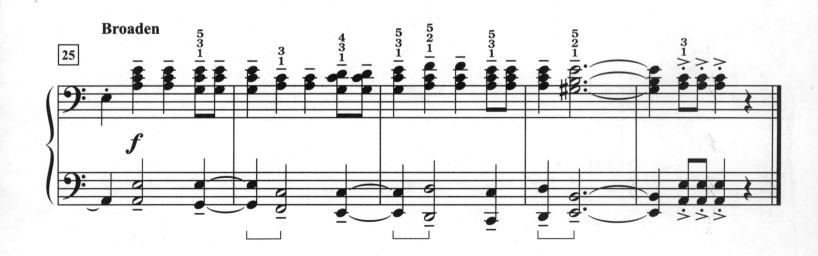

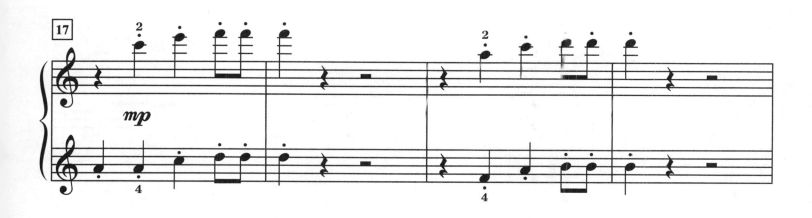

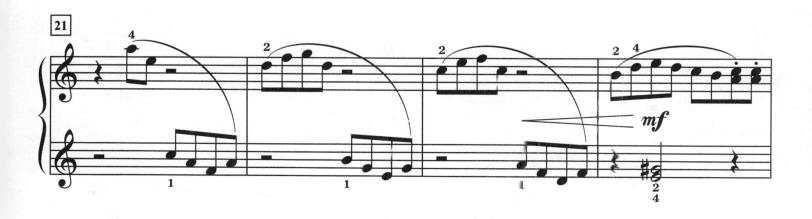

Samba brasileiro

"Brazilian Samba"

The samba has become a national symbol of the Brazilian Carnival. The style is felt in two with playful, driving energy. The piano *montuno* is popular in many styles of Latin music (see m. 32).

Rhythm Workshop

Tap rhythm 3x daily.

mm. 50–51

Secondo

Wynn-Anne Rossi

Samba brasileiro

"Brazilian Samba"

The samba has become a national symbol of the Brazilian Carnival. The style is felt in two with playful, driving energy. The piano *montuno* is popular in many styles of Latin music (see m. 30).

Rhythm Workshop

Tap rhythm 3x daily.

mm. 46–47

Primo

Wynn-Anne Rossi

Secondo